The Great East Japan Earthquake

東日本大震災

3．11

Thanks for the support from the United States and the the world,
Thank you for Operation Tomodachi

渋谷　知美

(Shibuya Tomomi)

3.11 Tomomi Shibuya

Nobody had imagined that such a day would come…Dogs, cats, stones, sands, grasses, trees, oceans, mountains,
my husband, my parents, my children, and I also had never imagined.

9th March , Heisei 23(2011), about
2:00 p.m.
When I was in my friend's house, a magnitude 5 earthquake occurred. My friend's house was about 200 meters away from my house toward the seaside. There, two of my friends and 3 children of ours and I, six people were enjoying a tea break. It shook hard. Quite a while since the last one.
Then a tsunami attention warning was given.
"What to do? Evacuate?"
Now the memory of our conversation comes back.

Of course, we didn't, and resumed our tea break.

Yamamoto town, Watari county, Miyagi prefecture,my hometown.
It's the southernmost of Miyagi prefecture and there, it doesn't snow a lot, and the climate is mild, so it is called "The Shounan of Miyagi". Hokki shellfish (Sakhalin surf clam), apples, and strawberries are its special products, and there live about 16,000 people.
It is considered to be a commuting area to Sendai, and it's a satellite town where people don't pass each other during the daytime.
Because of its warm climate and little snow, not a few people move to the town after retirement.
I have lived there 35 years without thinking whether I love this town or not, but I have been thinking that I would live in this town all my life.
My husband whom I had met in Fukusima, has married into my family in

Yamamoto town, there were six people in my family, my husband, father, mother, and 2 daughters, and it was a typical three generation family for this town. We had a main building, a shed, and a 4 space parking lot, a field, and a garden. The ground was spacious, and gave us enough distance from the neighbors. The Neighboring association is called "Tonarigumi", we attend on each other's ceremonial occasions. A circular notice made a community, and often neighbors stayed in my house from morning to evening. The door was always left unlocked, except the day to go far all day. The life is peaceful and quiet without any serious accidents.
I had never thought the sea was so near, my life was so near to the sea, until that event happened.

I have lived with the sea since I was a child. My mother's parents' house was in Watari town, neighboring town of Yamamoto town, and just near to the seawall. I remember that I sometimes felt the sound of the wave terrible, sometimes comfortable. When I went there, I have played walking around the pine wood with my elder sister and cousins. Now I recall that it was a pine woods called "tsunami control forest"
It was very mysterious place for us. Inside was dim, and there, the strange trees and plants had grown thick. In my vague memory, there was a small puddle, and I killed a crawfish, then caught another with the meat of the first one.
I often went swimming in the sea.
I used to go and come back in a swimsuit, sometimes by bicycle.
The sea was very gentle and comfortable.
I had always felt lucky to have been born near the sea. I would wash a tomato and a cucumber in the sea and ate with its salty taste. Once I brought a pot of hot water, and made an instant noodle and ate it, or I collected sea shells alone. I really often went to the sea. I would just say to my family, "I'm going to the

sea" and go out, they would never stopped me. Watching the wave, I thought, "This wave connects to the world", and I was lost in thought. My heart calmed down when I was watching the sea, and I could fully enjoy the feeling of "the creature" living on the earth. I really loved the sea. I remember when I became adolescent, I dated with my boyfriend on the seaside. There we shared laughter acting dramatically, my life was always with the sea.

And yet, why such a thing did happen? Why the tsunami was so big, and destroyed everything, all the things we had until then?

11th March, Heisei 23 ,2:48 p.m.

"Get out!"
"Get out!"
My chief was waving his hand upward.
"Get out? Why?"

2:00 p.m. of Friday.
It was the time for 50- minute-swimming coach, from 1:30 p.m.
Friday, I worked until 3:30 p.m. as a part-timer of the swimming school.
"After Friday, it will be a holiday tomorrow. Hang on," I thought.
Probably because of the cold weather, there were only two students instead of five on that day, so I was coaching in a relaxed mood.
I had got to work, and since November, 2010 I worked in the swimming school in the neighboring town, three times a week, from 10:00 a.m. to 3:30 p.m. as a part-timer. A half year had passed and I just got used to the job.
"Get out!"
"Get out!"
The chief was sending a sign to me from the shower room, which was about 2

meters apart from the pool. The next moment, my body swung widely from side to side and the water of the pool splashed against the poolside violently.
I was holding two children in my arms and concentrated on their safety.
"A cloud of dust?"
Concrete pieces of the ceiling fell down one after another.
A cloud of concrete? They fell into the water and on the poolside wildly, and smoke stirred up.
Holding the children, I got out of the pool. I heard a scream. In the back lane, an exercise class for back pain was taking place, and around 20 women aged from 50's to 80's were there. There was another swimming class for children, around five children were there. My right eye vaguely caught the sight of everyone heading the emergency exit on the right side.
I went to the shower room where the chief was. I was thinking about my children while holding two children in my arms.
My elder child should have been at the kindergarten. I expected that the teachers guided the children to the safe place. The younger one, my parents were taking care of her.
"Please, they never went to the store and took an elevator." I prayed.
Shaking. Still shaking.
Concrete pieces of the ceiling were continuously falling, and screams of somebody didn't stop. In the cloud of dust, I could see slightly that two women couldn't get out of the swimming pool. But holding the children, I could do nothing.
"What comes next?" I asked the chief.
"Falling. The ceiling is going to fall!"
The chief answered.
Shaking. Shaking violently.
A horrible sound. Have never heard such a sound, a rattle, or a clamor. And a cloud of dust, screams.
"It's all over. I don't want to die!"

I was barely on my feet, holding the children, my body swayed from side to side widely.
"Please open the door over there, now!" I shouted.
There was an emergency exit door about 2 meters away on the right side. I saw the chief run vigorously, and keep the door open.
Just thinking, "I will protect these children!"
I ran.
The emergency exit was unexpectedly high from the ground, I recognized it after jumping down. My steps got shaky, and I handed over the boy to the chief. My heart was pounding, and the children were crying.

There was an earthquake two days ago, and a visitor and I talked about evacuation.
It must be unpleasant if we have to evacuate in a swimsuit."
We were joking.
Only the employees had taken a fire drill. Though the Off-Miyagi Earthquake was expected, we had hardly done anything.
We were not prepared for an earthquake disaster at all.
The Off-Miyagi Earthquake. At that time I was 3 years old. And I remember vaguely that it was an uproar. I don't think that I have specifically received a disaster prevention education afterwards.
I didn't have an opportunity to receive an education about how to live, or how to survive. Also I didn't have an opportunity to know the violence of nature and didn't know that we must escape from nature when it uses violence against human beings, either. I didn't know the time was drawing near for the people in Japan, people in the world to learn that human being are so powerless, can't do anything.
And at this time, definitely, there were still a lot of human lives beating hearts on the coast.

As everybody said later,
"If only the tsunami had not come ... if only an earthquake..."
Everybody was still alive at that moment…
After getting out through the emergency exit, I was guided by the staff of the Bus administration office in the next building to stand back several meters from the building. I let the child sit down, and went to take back another child from the chief who were guiding people at the door. From the emergency exit, the women of the exercise class, staggering, like in a pile, escaped one after another, it was the first time for them to jump down from the high emergency exit, someone skinned a knee, and was bleeding.
Everybody was agitated. With a pounding heart, I was intending to hand over the two children to their parent safely. Nobody stayed calm, and every face was rigid.
Shaking, shaking. Strong aftershocks continued even after we went outside in a swimsuit.
"The ground may split open, and we may fall into the split."
I had an image like S.F., and prayed for the safety of my family.
At the place away from the main entrance of the facility, the employees spread a blue seat. Everybody was led there, and I could hand over the children to their parents. The children were agitated and crying. After settling the visitors on the blue seat, then we decided to move into the school bus together. Everybody was shivering from the cold with the wet body in swimsuit. There, at every aftershock, screams still broke out. There was a long line of the traffic jam on the national road which ran beside the facility. I knew intuitionally that traffic lights were out.
I felt many driver’s eyes, but I didn’t have time to care about it. We started the engines of two buses, and led the people onto each bus. The parents who had been on the stands, the visitors who had been in the locker room, and the staff, there supposed to be around 50 people in all.

The manager gave the staff instructions to lead them into the bus and calm them down. The parents who met their children left for home by car one after another without even changing their clothes.
Shaking, shaking. The staffs were handed the helmets, and ordered to bring the visitor's clothes and valuables from the building to the bus. The visitors, wrapping towels around the body, changed the clothes in the bus. At the end, the staffs were allowed to pick up personal belongings and change the clothes.
Inside the bus was extremely disordered. An elderly woman who had a weak heart was apparently upset. Everybody was agitated.
Shaking, shaking. I thought if the building collapsed as soon as I entered it, I couldn't come back alive.
But I still wanted to pick up my valuables and go home to confirm the safety of my family as soon as possible. Putting on a helmet I entered the building, and saw the office messed up, showing how violently it had shaken. Desks and papers were scattered and it was not the office which I saw only 30 minutes ago, before the lesson. With a beating heart, I headed for the locker room to pick up my stuff before another shock. I had a very strange feeling, and I didn't know what I was doing. My hands might be shaking and I wanted to relieve my throbbing heart at any rate.
I took my things and returned to the bus and changed my own clothes. Radio was playing in the bus, but most of it was noise, I couldn't hear well. However I still remember someone's words clearly.
"They say Sendai Airport is flooded!"
I don't know who said it, but those were the words I couldn't understand at all.
"What is he saying?"
"Sendai Airport is flooded?"
This was the first information of the tsunami I got. Nobody on the bus connected the meaning of the flooded with "tsunami". Everybody was saying, "Why? Why the airport is flooded?"
Outside, it was sun-showering and raindrops were hitting the windows.

Later, the media repeatedly reported how all people in Japan had been spending that time.

"After an earthquake, it often rains, doesn't it?"

With a throbbing heart, I heard a working student talking.

The employees were ordered to drive each visitor home.

In the bus, everyone was making a call by mobile phone, and I tried to call my family many times, too. By chance, I could get a call from my father.

"Are you all right? A tsunami arrived our house. We took shelter in Yamashita Daiichi Elementary School. Come here, but no hurry".

He said.

"A tsunami arrived our house?"

"A tsunami arrived our house?"

What was he saying?

Our house was at least 2 kilometers away from the sea. And also on its seaside, there was a railroad, and of course it was a railroad embankment.

"Washed over it, a tsunami arrived?"

It was beyond all imagination.

"I see. Everybody is all right, isn't it?"

I confirmed that my father, my mother, and two children had evacuated together and was relieved for the present.

5:00 p.m. The part-timers were told to break up.

"About the work after tomorrow, I will contact you later".

The manager said.

Nobody knew what was going on at that time. Everybody thought that we could soon make contact and go back to the normal life, nobody imagined that communication means, food, gasoline would be gone.

Then I got into my car.

My heart was still pounding. Shaking, still shaking.

The radio was repeating information that a traffic light fell down at an intersection in Sendai or something like that. Though the radio was on, my

ears, my eyes, my brain were confused that I couldn't understand well.
Human imagination can be made only through experiences. Now I can tell.
"What happened? What should I do?"
I didn't know whether my brain was working or not. That was the feeling mixed with uneasiness and excitement that I had never experienced before.
It was hard to accept.
"I must calm down. Calm down."
I said to myself, in vain.
The roads were terribly deformed. They cracked in some places, and here and there, walls fell down, houses collapsed.
Without traffic lights the national road had a heavy traffic jam.
"What should I do? What should I do…?"
I was repeating in my mind.
"A tsunami arrived our house. Everybody is in the shelter."
My father's words flashed in my mind many times.
"Probably I cannot go home today. I had better buy food and drink."
I thought, that my children would get hungry in the evening. And I decided to drop by the convenience store. However, there was a long line in front of it.
The inside was dim because of power failure, and customers lined up to the outside.
"With such a long line, I can't buy anything."
I gave up and passed it.
Furthermore, I became impatient with the traffic jam, and took a bypath. It was a road between fields which runs between the national road and sea.

There was not a traffic jam, and I speeded up the car. Then I saw there was a puddle.
"What's that? Subsidence?"
I went through the water, then the road turned normal again. But after driving for a while, it was flooded again.

I was scared, but I could see other cars around, so didn't think to return and went on.
I approached an elevated bridge over a railroad. It was a very high bridge and from there, usually I could see the sea side of Watari town.
The strawberry fields, the green houses, JR Jo-Ban Line, the seaside landscape.
It was shining. It was not the landscape I always saw.
There was a lot of water, and it was shining against the sunset. The town was covered with water and there was no sign of inhabitants.
Anyhow, water was shining. The flooded houses and buildings made me feel the silent atmosphere even from inside of the car.
"What happened? Why is the town flooded, too?"
I couldn't understand at all.
After passing down the elevated bridge, I had to drive into even deeper pool, making the sound of splash, splash I didn't know how deep it was, I realized there were no car to be seen anywhere. The car's body sank into the water rapidly. Then a few men wearing a happi coat like a fire company's happi were standing on the road. They were sending me a signal to go up toward mountain side.
With the car soaked in the water, I slowed down and opened the window.
"This road is closed, go up toward the national road."
They said.
I headed the car toward the mountain side.
The sun was setting, and it was a bumpy road with no traffic light, traffic jam was horrible. On the side of the road, houses collapsed, and block walls fell down. At the unusual scene, I got more impatient.
"Please let my family be safe. Please let me meet them safely." I hold the steering tightly, the radio repeated many times the news that a signal in Sendai city fell down.
I arrived at Yamashita Daiich Elementary School which was the designated evacuation area of the district where I lived in, and about which I had heard on

my father's phone call. I'm not sure, but I guess it was after 5:30 p.m, about 40 cars parked in the school grounds. I met an acquaintance at the gate, and talked with him through the opened car-window.

"None of my family has come. You don't know, do you?"

He said. He was my neighbor who lived several meters away from my house.

"I'm afraid I don't know. I could speak to my father on the phone by chance, and heard that they are here."

I said.

"I see. I'll go anyway."

He said so and drove away.

I entered the school grounds and found out my family's car. My mother and two daughters were in, the elder daughter, 5 years old, a senior kindergartener, the younger one, 18 months. I was relieved to confirm their safety. And I hoped my husband would come here from Sendai safely.

I saw my neighbor.

"He has come to the shelter, too…"

I thought absentmindedly without knowing what happened. My father came back from the store which located several hundred meters away from the school with some mandarin oranges and dried potatoes.

"Maybe still nobody thought of, it wasn't crowded. I bought what they had, a bit heavy food. Let the children eat."

He said.

According to my parents when they let the younger daughter take a nap, that first shock hit them. Immediately they held the child and went to the outside. When they came back most of the furniture remained intact. Then the disaster prevention radio gave a tsunami warning, they decided to evacuate at once, because they were taking care of their grandchild. (Later, they also said that they might have heard it from the fire company's car for the public information, not from the disaster prevention radio of Yamamoto town) So it was before 4:00 p.m. that they evacuated to the elementary school, and there

were only four or five cars. However, when they were going to change her diaper, they became aware that they didn't bring any. So they went back home together to pick up diapers.
When they got into the car with diapers and baby wipes, and looked both way to get on to the road from the house, from right (east) side (the sea side), they saw the black water close in on them at great speed.
My mother shouted to my father who was driving the car,
"Hurry up!"
Watching the black water in the back mirror, he stepped on the accelerator and for dear life, escaped to the school. Water was flowing very fast, they said.
On the way, they happened to come across the elder daughter's kindergarten bus and saw it was going to turn to the sea side, my father got out of the car and desperately tried to stop the bus gesturing "Don't turn! Don't turn!"

Then he explained the circumstances, and took over the elder daughter.
I repeatedly tried to call my husband, and finally could contact him.
He was heading here, too.
My older sister came to the shelter alone. She told us that she couldn't get in touch with her daughter so she was going to the town office anyway. She brought my children some snacks and drinks she had at home.
My niece was 5years old and in the middle grade of the kindergarten.
Her kindergarten was in the direction of the sea side.
My heart was still beating fast. Before I knew, it was getting dark around there.
It was cold. And still shaking.
At every shock, my heartbeat got faster. I took my children's hands and said,
"It's all right",
I was saying it to myself. It was very cold. I kept the engine running to make inside warm, but I was scared that we'd run out of gas before the morning. The indicator was showing '1', usually I filled it up on every weekend, and that day was Friday, one day before filling day, so there left a little. We had to

stay together in my father's car. But it was so crowded, and the children got bored, too.

So we moved into the gymnasium. There were two or so heaters, and some private electric generators. But people were all around there, and there was no place to stand. Of course, no place to sit. Anyhow, it was cold.

I saw an acquaintance, and exchanged a few words. A person nearby gave some chocolate to my children, I was grateful for her kindness. Everybody was extremely uneasy, felt like crying, not knowing what happened. At every aftershock, everybody was

stirred, and voices like scream broke out.

I went to the restroom with my child. It was totally dark. Here and there, primary school children and junior high school students holding lights like flashlight were standing with adults. At the entrance of the restroom, a bucket which contained some water was handed. The water in the bucket was drawn from the swimming pool. Inside the restroom, the condition was terrible. Wasted sanitary napkins were scattered, and diapers for adults were rolled up and put aside. Even after flash water, it smelled intensely.

In the dim lights, we used the toilet.

We gave up spending night in the gymnasium and returned to the car. Then my husband finally arrived from Sendai. I think that it was around 7:00 p.m., and six people spent night in my father's car, my father on the driver's seat, my mother on the passenger seat, and making the two rear seats flat, my husband, I, and two children, four people there. I gave my children some snacks, dried potatoes, and mandarin oranges, and let them sleep as flat as possible. Listening to the radio, I didn't know whether I was awake or asleep, anyway, such uneasy times continued. The body was very tired and sometimes I closed my eyes. Then it shook, an aftershock came. Through the window on the left, I could see the two-story school building towering white and big.

"If that building falls down, what to do?"

I thought. Radio was sending information one after another.
"In XX shopping center, X people seem to got injured."
"XX Kindergarten, everybody is safe."
"XX nursery, everybody is safe."
"XX, everybody sheltered in a house nearby."
"XX, please help. SOS."

I could tell that a person was reading news in tears.
"Everybody, a little more patience. Please hold on. The tsunami will be coming again and again, as the second wave, the third wave. Please never approach the mouth of the river or the coast. The expected arrival time of the next tsunami is X:00, . At Sendai Bay, it is expected to be 8 meters high!"
My heart was pounding.
I couldn't understand what was happening at all, and I had never heard the word 'tsunami' so many times at a time.
They said,
"A fire seems to break out in Watari town."
From this elementary school which stood on the hill, we could see the flame on the leftward seaside.
Listening to the radio, I opened and closed my eyes repeatedly. It was a cold night, I could see stars clearly. Snow was fluttering, and it was getting even colder.
I think it was about 11:00 p.m. the news came from the radio.
"There is information that in Sendai Arahama, nearby Shiogama-Watari Line, 200 to 300 dead bodies were found."
I couldn't believe my ears.
"What? Why 200 to 300 dead bodies were found around the road in Arahama by earthquake? what…?"
All at once, I got goose bumps.
"Oh my god!"

I remember that my mother and I shouted.
I couldn't understand at all. On the road, dead bodies. The information was coming from the radio repeatedly afterwards. It was totally dark night, and even a siren or the sound of ambulance wasn't heard. It was such a dark night that I couldn't remember a life where we have electricity.
"I have never thought, but actually, night is so dark…"
I listened to the radio for a while, and was worried about my niece. And my grandmother.
She lived with my mother's younger brother and his wife, and their children, 6 people in total. Her house was near the sea, just beside the embankment. She was over 80 years old, and stayed at home alone in the daytime. As she begun to show signs of dementia, they sent her to a day care facility three times a week. The facility was near the sea, too. On that day, Friday, too, she was there. It was a day care facility close to the fishing port of TorinoUmi in Watari town. In the next building, there was a hot spring facility of 5 stories.
"Dozens of people seem to take refuge in TorinoUmi Hot Spring facility in Watari town."
Hearing from the radio, we talked,
"She must be taken to the hot spring. Her diaper may be full."
The niece was second grade of the kindergarten which was not very near to the sea, maybe 2 to 3 kilometers away from the sea. According to the information from the radio, the children of that kindergarten and the nearby nursery seemed to have sheltered in the second floor of a house nearby.
"What on the earth is going on…?"
At every information I couldn't believe my ears. I hadn't had such an experience that I listened to the radio and couldn't picture the situation. It was a shock, and yet I couldn't imagine anything. It had never happened before, and all I felt was uneasiness, while my heart pounding.
I dozed a little and woke up. I remember that I looked at the watch at 12:00 at midnight and 4:00 in the early morning.

"Was my house carried away, too? My room, my clothes, my bags, and my goods, they have disappeared, too? The house crumbled? Or was carried away?"

While thinking such things, I wondered how my niece and grandmother were feeling in the refuge.

"Staying inside the car with the engine running, it's still so cold, the outside must be freezing tonight."

I thought.

On the radio, a woman was repeating the announcement with a tearful trembling voice. "On the roof parking lot of XX, there are 50 to 60 neighbors. We don't have food nor water. It's cold. Please help."

"Several hundred people are on the roof of the XX schools. Some people are injured. Please help."

"XX nursery school, all the members are safe. We will spend tonight in the nursery school. Please pick them up tomorrow."

"On the roof of XX store, dozens of people took refuge. Please help. It's cold. Some people are still wet."

"I am in the second floor of XX. I heard the next tsunami is expected to be 8 meters high. If really comes 8 meters one next, I will be washed away. I'm scared. Please help."

"There are dozens of people on the roof of XX. Sendai Bay complex became a sheet of fire. Flame is approaching. I'm scared. Without stopping, it is approaching rapidly. Only several hundred meters to reach here. Please help."

The broadcast was repeated without a break.

I didn't understand what was going on, just tears streamed down one after another.

It was a dark, deep night and in the sky, stars were shinning.

"Everybody, a little more patience. Please don't give up and hold on. Everybody, the day will break soon. The Self-Defense Force is coming to rescue you. Please, everybody, let's join forces and get over this night. The temperature in Sendai is falling. Keep yourselves warm with newspapers or towels as possible as you can. Everybody, a little more patience!"

Her tearful, but powerful voice tore my heart even more.
"Now, there was a magnitude 4 earthquake, supposed to be an aftershock. Please secure your safety. All of you, please calm down."
"The tsunami comes over and over. It sweeps as the first wave, the second wave. Everybody, please never approach the dangerous places."
"The expected arrival time of the next tsunami is X o'clock. Sendai Bay 8 meters, X bay X meter. X fishing port X meter."
Listening to such a repetition of the radio, in the car with the engine running, I sometimes moved my body a little, sometimes stroked the children's shoulders who were about to awake. Before I knew the sky was brightening slightly. When I went outside, my legs and back were aching.
In the school grounds, more than 50 cars lined up. Everybody kept the engine running. From the school grounds I looked the direction of my house, but couldn't see anything in particular.
It was getting light rapidly. I think that it was past 9:00 a.m., the principal appeared and told us.
"We are going to distribute rice balls. Please come and take them. We made them with the rice which neighbors gave us kindly. There are facilities for providing meals in this elementary school. Everybody, please bring your ingredients."
I stood in line and waited for my turn. There seemed to be 60 to 70 people.
A person still wearing her uniform, maybe an office worker, a person still wearing his school uniform, maybe a student, a person wearing his work clothes, a person wearing his suit.
"Everybody is wearing the same clothes since yesterday."
I thought.
Their hair was unkempt, and the makeup had come off. Everybody was so

tired, and, had the expression hard to describe, which was showing their uneasiness and their feeling that they had no place to turn to.
Pure white rice. They were just wrapped in cling wrap, and rounded. We had two each. Everybody sat in front of the school building and ate the rice balls. I gave to my children, too.
They didn't understand this unusual situation, ate the rice balls with a happy expression as if they came to a festival.
And again, that expression tightened my chest.
"A day different from yesterday begins."
I felt intuitionally. It was a morning as if we had declared war. I was afraid that Japan, or the whole world was going to fight against something. Watching the children eating the rice balls, I swore to myself, like a parent of the wartime,
"I don't know what will happens from now on, but. I will raise my children at any cost."
While I was eating, a person whose clothes was muddy under his chest walked up. He was a man of 70's, and his expression was timid. A woman approached him and talked something. And then she supported him with her arm around him, and guided to somewhere.
"Why he is muddy like that? Why his clothes are dirty like that? Because of the tsunami? What on the earth is a tsunami? So severe that we can't escape?
Can't it be safe if we go up to the high place? I wonder where he was last night?
What did he do? How did he get so muddy that his clothes changed the color?"
Knowing nothing, my mind was filled with questions.
I didn't know where it came from, I saw the extra newspaper.
The picture of the tsunami was on the front page. It was a picture of the sea spray which was higher than a pine wood.
"Such a thing had really happened… Is this the picture of the event that

happened in this region where we live?"
I couldn't believe it. On that day's newspaper, there was the scene of a collapsed building in Sendai city. Looking back now, most of information was about the earthquake.
After a while, the neighboring friend's family walked up in six people. Their feet were muddy, and they carried baggage as many as they could carry in their arms and on their back. Their appearance was full of fatigue, and I couldn't help running up to them and cried. My friend cried, too.
"Good to know you are safe! I have not seen you, I was really worried. We talked that you might go to the junior high school."
I said.
"Yeah, since the tsunami came, we were staying on the second floor. The tsunami reached right up to the second floor. Four cars were all carried away, but morning came, we decided to walk to the elementary school in six people."

Her father in law, her mother in law, her husband, 3-year and 1-year-old children. Their appearance was awfully worn out, as if they had come back from a battlefield. I couldn't even imagine what a night they spent, and how was the tsunami. More uneasiness and fear filled my heart.
Suddenly my father and husband said that they were going to walk to our house. My mother and I objected strongly because the tsunami warning was not canceled, and we didn't know when the next tsunami would come.
"Everybody is coming in muddy clothes. Fortunately, we were saved, but what will you do if a tsunami comes!"
But they didn't listen saying,
"It will be all right."
From somewhere a rumor that "Houses were broken into" spread out. Certainly the property like bankbook was just left in the house, no wonder that money was stolen. My husband and father decided to go saying that anyway

they would go and have a look of our house.
The principal of the elementary school called out to announce the arrival of the distribution again, and I lined up. The lunch was one piece of cookie.
"There are facilities for providing meals in this school. If we have ingredients, we can make anything. Please, everybody, offer some ingredients."
The principal was shouting. His face was worn out, too.
At the breakfast, there was the offer of ingredients. But the neighbors near the hill seemed to have quitted to offer hurriedly, sensing that it was not sure how long this situation would last.
"We can't stay here with one piece of cookie. Thinking about children, I can't."
I determined firmly.
My older sister came to inform us about my niece, and brought us some snacks. She told us that her daughter was rescued miraculously from the kindergarten bus which was caught in the tsunami, and spent night with wet body on the second floor of the kindergarten. Mud was even in her ear. And she had seen the all of the unfortunate happenings.

The elementary school was confused awfully.
"Didn't you see my father? I can't find him."
My classmate said.
"Mr. X is not seen. Where is he?"
Everyone was asking. A person who walked all night from Sendai asked,
"I couldn't go back home because the tsunami came. My wife is nowhere to be seen. I thought that she had come here, haven't you see her?"
He looked like he was going to burst into tears. It was a world where everything was unreal and unexpected. My heart was beating fast and I kept getting depressed.
I wonder how much time had passed, my husband and father came back. Their bottoms were muddy up to the knees.

“It’s terrible. The house is there. The bankbooks, too. The rooms of the second floor remain intact. The tsunami reached a few steps of the stairs from the first floor.”

My husband said he heard that The Self-Defense Force had been clearing the road first of all, and that dead bodies had been wrapped and carried out one after another. He said there was a corpse behind our house, too.

A tsunami into our house? A corpse behind our house? The word ‘corpse’, I have heard it only on the television or movies.

“What a world? My familiar house, the neighboring scenery, how have they changed? ” Only imagination and uneasiness flitted through my mind.

From the school grounds, cars disappeared one by one. People decided to go to their relatives or acquaintances’ house, and drove out. The older brother of my friend who had come here on foot in the morning, came to pick them up from Sendai.

“I’m sorry. We will go to my parents' house in Sendai. So Sorry…”

She said and cried.

She was just about my age, a mother of a 1-year-old child. She knew how terrible it is to stay in a shelter and that we did not have a place to go, and gave us several plastic bottles of tea which her older brother had brought. Families with children and pregnant women who arrived last night went away one after another, too. Most of my relatives live near the coast, so we had no place to go. However, when evening came, it seemed to be hard for six of us to spend night in the car in 6 people like last night. The gasoline was getting short, and we had no food to give our children.

I asked my mother,

“I want to let the children sleep flat tonight at least. Isn’t there any good place?”

She said that we could try to go to my grandmother’s brother’s house.

“I think, the tsunami did not reach there. But it must be annoying if six people go to their house uninvited, we will remain in the elementary school. ”

She said.

I was worried about my father, because he had an operation for a small cerebral thrombosis just one week ago and needed to rest.

We ran the car with remaining small amount of gasoline, and, my husband, two children and I, four of us headed for the aunt's house. My parents decided to stay at a friend's house.

When we arrived her house, the evacuees were just us, but other people evacuated too one after another. They were the relatives who had spent the night on the roof of the school, and had been rescued by a helicopter. I spent time there with the people I had never seen.

Everyone had spent a night like a nightmare. They said that they saw with their own eyes, a person who had been washed away, a person who had been waiting for help while holding onto a tree.

As I feared, the restroom got dirty first of all. Including us 13 people were staying. But my uncle and aunt were warm people, treated us kindly.

"You can eat anything. Clean the bottom of the child with remaining hot water of the bath. I will boil water with an oil stove."

My 18-month daughter who had not taken a bath, got a diaper rash.

I appreciated the hot water very much. I was sick for a bath. After getting out of the swimming pool, my body was dry and itchy. The head was itchy, too. And I felt sick with my teeth.

"What will become of us?"

With uncomfortable body and depressed feeling, only such a thought was growing in my mind.

Food was getting short rapidly. With various ideas, my aunt made noodle and rice cakes for us. Of course there was no water so we had to go to the town hall on foot to get the distributed water.

Fortunately we could use propane gas there. I was really thankful for their warmth. However, I knew that she looked at the empty refrigerator in the

kitchen, and that there were also their children's families. I was sorry for them that they accepted distant relatives like us without knowing until when.
Then, there came the information that my grandmother seemed to have been sent back home from the day care center. It was said that, as the earthquake was that big, they decided to send the visitors back home. If nobody was at home, then sent to the relative's. We had been convinced that she had taken refuge in the upper floor of the next building. Without telecommunication, a rumor had become the most reliable information. We concluded that she asked them to let her get off at the relative's house which locates 2 kilometers nearer than our house. I had heard that she had once stayed their house before.
The people who sent her was confused too, usually they would confirm by telephone, but on that day, she was sent to that relative's somehow.
I heard that the neighbors gathered in the relative's house, and they decided to evacuate in two cars, with their son who had returned from his work, and the children who were high school students. They said that someone saw the car which was carrying my grandmother get caught in the tsunami on their way. And there was a person who was looking for her son and his wife. So my parents and my mother's younger brother and his wife went to the police and were informed that most of the dead bodies which were found in Watari were sent to the gymnasium of the high school locating in an inland area, beyond the mountain, which was used for a morgue.
Afterwards, they identified my grandmother. There they knew that the people who evacuated with her, my grandmother's niece who drove a car, her child (a male high school student), his grandmother, and my grandmother had been caught in a tsunami together. They said that when the tsunami had come my grandmother had told them,
"Don't mind us, and get out." Her niece and the son tried to save two old women, but they couldn't. They themselves were washed away too, but fortunately they could climb on to the roof of a house, and spent the night with wet body.

My mother, hearing the story, said crying.
“I’m relieved to hear that. She was not alone, met her last moment with them. If she had been sent to our house, she would have been washed away alone.
My mother talked before that she remembered when Chile Earthquake occurred, goats and other animals of which people took care at home were washed away.

As to the fate to live in the seaside, as to my grandmother who lost her life because of a tsunami, my mother said in this way.
“She had a good last moment. I think she was happy.”
Watching her saying so, I couldn’t say anything.
We decided to leave for my husband’s parents' house in Fukushima where there seemed to be water, electricity, and gas. We had seen the picture of the explosion of Fukushima Daiichi Nuclear Power Station on the newspaper. On the one hand I thought that in such a place, if my children are exposed to radiation in the future it will be a terrible story. But on the other hand, even though we didn’t have a place to go, I still wanted to get rid of the uncomfortableness of the body as possible, and sleep flat, blush the teeth….
In four people, we headed Fukushima, where his parents live. On the way, using the remaining few battery of the mobile phone, we could connect with them, and knew lifeline was secured. Though a gas station had a long line, we could manage to fill it. Everybody was exhausted. Being able to take a bath and sleep on a mattress every day, what a happiness. Blush the teeth, eat meal, everything seemed to be a remote past. We were awfully tired.
In Fukushima, we did not go out at all, and every day wore a mask. From now on where would we live? My husband had decided to change his job a little before the earthquake, but after the earthquake, he got a notice of the cancellation from the new work place. His position of the former work had expired, so he was unemployed. The elder daughter was expected to enter an elementary school.

I talked with my husband many times, but there was no way to live in my parents' house. In the place where once tsunamis came, we could never be relieved. And besides, we did not want our children to have this painful feeling. We looked for an apartment while living in Fukushima.

In Watari town, the neighboring town of Yamamoto town where we had lived until then, we could find an apartment through my acquaintance. We moved there just before the day of the entrance ceremony of the elementary school. In Watari town that was a stricken area, the entrance ceremony, usually held at the end of April, had been postponed.

We had trouble getting household appliances, because stores were not open. We managed to prepare household effects to start a new life. As the school was used for a shelter, the entrance ceremony was briefly held in the hall of the facility for children next to the school. Many people were wearing everyday clothes. A person who lost her husband, a child who lost his parents, and everyone attended with mixed feeling, it was such a ceremony.

In May, the cremation of my grandmother was finally held. Everyone's mourning clothes were also washed away, it was a simple ceremony of cremation. We were lucky to be able to reserve a crematorium, while there were dozens of people buried as temporary burial.

They said that the dead body of my grandmother was neat because it was found comparatively early. However, my mother said to me that it had better not to let the children do the last parting. The face of the grandmother was totally different from "the dead person's" face I have seen before. It looked like an artificial one, and I thought that she had fought so hard to the very end.

"It must be very painful for her. I wonder how much black muddy water she did swallow."

The funeral services were held one after another, and at the end everybody was handed a small plastic bag which looked like a shopping bag of a supermarket. In that bag, there were the muddy black clothes which my grandmother was wearing on that her last day. Those were the clothes of my grandmother who got into the day care center's car as usual, experienced that shake with everyone, and was caught by the black waves. There was a family whose member, four or five people were all cremated together.

I think it was getting more like spring. From that day, everyday had passed with dizzying speed, while I didn't know what was going on.

Misfortune of friends, misfortune of people who lost their husband, misfortune of people who lost their child, and news of complete destruction of friends' houses. That man, this woman, everybody was in the middle of misfortune.

Nobody had imagined but someone can't be seen any more after that day. Even if you look for, and look for harder, you can't find him. For families of deceased whose body was still not found out, only time was passing in vain. While such people were side by side, schools began, works began, water and gas became available, the life had been repeated steadily.

People who repairs their original houses, people who enter the temporary houses then build their new houses, and people who live in deemed-temporary housings like me.

After that day, I, maybe everybody in Japan, have learnt "nothing can be absolute" Even now, when I look at the tsunami's arrival spot on the coast and it's extent,

I can't believe that day. What a terrible thing has happened — we are spending time while holding disconsolate feeling. Anytime when we look back, we feel that we are still in that night. When I go to bed, the last face of my grandmother comes to my mind. And also relatives, friends, acquaintances who are gone, the landscape of the town, the view of the houses, and the life, the seaside living.

Soon I will greet the third New Year after the earthquake disaster in the temporary housing. In these three years, I lost many things, and always feel sad.

Now I take a part-time job related to the earthquake disaster and now I happened to be helping with the reconstruction work of Yamamoto town. Having experienced the earthquake disaster, I strongly wish that first of all, people living on a coast never have the same feeling as us, even after one hundred, one thousand years has passed.

When a great disaster as big as this happened, I want you to make sure to evacuate and save your life, and inherit some “form”, by which nobody lose their life in a disaster.

I wish as one living creature on the earth that everyone respects "protection of life" as the most important thing. Even 1,000 years, 2000 years later…

~ Afterword~

On the newspaper, I saw an advertisement of "call for article about the Great East Japan Earthquake." It is mentioned that "in order to leave the memories of the Great East Japan Earthquake to future generations." The application conditions required more than 50 pieces of manuscript paper. As I get sucked into the job and housework everyday, I thought that I could not possibly apply and closed the newspaper. But the next day, I still couldn't get over and opened the newspaper again.

"I want to try!"

If I write down what I experienced, and if people of the future read it and know, on 2011.3.11, what kind of feeling one human being had....And if a person who read this manuscript 10 years, 20 years later, due to having read it, can save his life when a similar disaster happens ...I had such a thought at the back of my mind.

I don't want such a sad incident to happen again, never. I didn't see the black tsunami actually. That's why I thought I could tell people something with the same feeling of the people who has never seen a tsunami.

What a tsunami is like, how fast and strongly the tsunami carried away everything with its terrible speed and power...

I was really shocked when I saw the image of tsunami on the television or something. For the people who didn't know anything, it might be just an image of a tsunami surging upon. However, I can tell that inside the building there are my friends, relatives and acquaintances. I want you to remember that there was a person who took a picture in the distance, and also there was a person who fought desperately till the last moment in that building.

~Finally to Granma in the heaven~

Granma, thank you for everything.

A big tsunami came, and on the coast, almost everything was gone.

Our memorable house has completely disappeared, too.

The sea is not only beautiful, isn't it?

But I still treasure the memory that I played a lot in the beautiful sea.

Because I was happy spending time with everyone there.

And, I will never forget that you fought out till the last moment, forever.

Thank you Americans, and all the people around the world who have helped us.

"Kept alive — Gratitude toward the world for support"
Shibuya Tomomi

I have survived through the Great East Japan Earthquake, and after that started to receive various supports. World has supported Japan, and "TOHOKU", my hometown. "So thankful", I shed tears of gratitude as much as of grief over my sad experience in the earthquake. Everybody lives on this same earth. "Everybody lives on this same earth where something unexpected could happen."

I wonder when I started hearing the word 'Operation Tomodachi (Operation Friend)'. Lifeline has been cut since 11th March. There was no network for mobile phones, and after being out of battery they were not useful. Those were such days. I even couldn't pay attention to the information other than "someone's safety".

A few days later, I finally felt like watching news.

Familiar Sendai Airport has appeared in the TV. There were American soldiers whom I had only seen in films. There were hundreds of American well-built soldiers in camouflaged clothes. I remember it was on the news, that 'Operation Tomodachi' had been undertaken to clean up the Sendai Airport by American soldiers.

'Such a thing is happening right now…' It was so touching that my eyes were filled with tears.

Until then, I had been sad, suffering and bearing with the disaster that had happened to me, but 'Operation Tomodachi' on TV brought me to somewhere where I could see the broader picture, finding a way out from the deep depression of the earthquake.

After extended period of time since the earthquake, the word 'relief supplies' has become the part of our life. Well, it was not only the word. I have been surrounded by the relief goods.
Water, rice, canned food, prepared food, portable radios, rice bowls, kitchen goods, bicycles, clothes, underwear, shoes, diapers and donation… A wide variety of goods have been distributed as 'relief supplies'.

I visited every time when there was a notice of distribution from the government or local community. Sometimes I met a friend there and confirmed each other's safety. Sometimes foreigners provided me supplies and poured me a cup of tea. At that time, we had no idea how much money would be necessary for the resettlement. Choosing the things from supplies was enjoyable as if we were doing the shopping. I remember we were talking with smiles,
"It's very nice for a change."
There were expensive brand's handkerchiefs, the same clothes I was wearing before the earthquake, delicious foreign snacks which cannot be tasted unless we are traveling abroad. Those were something I haven't seen before. 'Relief supplies' have not only helped us materially, but also supported us mentally at present and for the future as 'warm kindness of the world.' This form of support has made me positive.

I had only been thinking, "Why such a sad thing happened…What will happen next?", but now I think,
"There are many supportive hands given to us passionately from the world. Happy! Grateful! World has been trying to save us."
Ironically, "Earthquake has connected the countries…"
Only after the sad thing occurred, I felt grateful for the kindness of people living in other countries. World has been watching over us, world has been

encouraging us. As one who has been allowed to live, this grateful feelings have become my resolution,
"I want to do something to show my gratitude someday!!"
War has been constantly rising somewhere in the world. We also have a sad history of war in Japan. I also heard that US army has appealed the importance of Futenma base for a rescue operation of the earthquake.

As one who suffered from the earthquake, I will deliver the fact of earthquake to my children. I will tell about the support from other countries, and 'Operation Tomodachi'. I want to tell that the fact that the people around world were focusing on us was the one of the reasons why we could be positive.
I believe that my children won't have a feeling of the earthquake as merely a "bad incident".
I believe it will be similar to my feeling of "world connecting to each other", "gratitude" and "wishing to express the gratitude someday", that kind of feeling.

For foreigners who distributed relief supplies and poured me a tea, for American soldiers who helped us clean up Sendai Airport as 'Operation Tomodachi', it should be the same as me. I wish each person will deliver the stern reality of Japan, Miyagi prefecture, Tohoku and the feeling of those who suffered with the earthquake, which they saw with their own eyes, to someone in some way.

I will tell my children about what I saw in the earthquake, and those who came to Japan to support us from other countries will talk to people around. I believe those will be linked someday, somewhere. I'm not sure how far in the future but somewhere, feelings toward 'the Great East Japan Earthquake' will connect each other, with my descendants and descendants of people around the world. How about imagining such a future…?

I will never forget the support we received from the countries around the world after the earthquake, as well as the earthquake itself. Those who passed away on that day would never know that there was a lot of support from other countries. It is the truth of the earthquake only known by those who have survived. I wish to express my gratitude someday in the future for sure. It is the fact of earthquake which I can convey because I'm alive. I strongly wish the sad memory of earthquake become one of the history which leads to connecting the world more peacefully.

Introduction of Content

Shaking very hard. Shaking wherever I go. My body and mind can't stay calm, but I need to act for the next thing. Unordinary view like some SF film jumps into my eyes, but I still need to think and move. This is what the evacuation is during a catastrophe. How do you protect yourself when you cannot stay calm? Let's think about the "importance of escaping" together.

About the Author

Tomomi Shibuya, born on 9th November, 1974 in Yamamoto town Watari-gun, Miyagi prefecture. 39 years old, female. She has a husband and two daughters (eight and four years old). She has suffered from the earthquake when she was living together with her parents and family (Six people in total). Now residing in deemed-temporary housing (regular properties the city rented to be used as temporary housing) in Watari-town next to Yamamoto-town. She was working at a swimming school three times a week as a part-time worker, but her workplace has been completely destroyed so she changed a job. Now she is involving in a reconstruction support work of Yamamoto-town as a part-time worker.

~ Book review~

We Japanese experienced a great earthquake disaster once in 1,000 years. There is my head family in Miyagi prefecture, and a large number of relatives live there. Miyagi is the second hometown for me. My relative suffered from this great earthquake disaster, too.

So it is not other people's affairs. My relative performed the debris processing of the stricken area by this great earthquake disaster.

I thought that there may be something that I could do to help them. So I went to the stricken area of Miyagi and decided to collect manuscripts about "the earthquake disaster" from Miyagi citizen of the prefecture. I asked Kahoku Shinpo Press and my wish was able to come true. When I read this work, I realized there was an unreported stern reality of evacuation and unbearable pain. Also I thought that it was a valuable, important work to leave in history. The words of the last "thought for grandmother" tightened my chest. We Japanese must not let this great earthquake disaster wear. A capital inland earthquake, the Nankai Trough Earthquake is expected to occur in the near future, too. Please read this manuscripts and imagine the feeling of disaster victims and situations. If you were the victim…?

The present, Japan has many problems. However, a Japanese citizen becomes one and will overcome it by all means. Finally I appreciate for all member and Kahoku Shinpo Press which cooperated for this plan. Thank you so much.

In Japan, Tohoku never loses. With a united effort, let's step forward confidently.

HIRO ENTERPRISE Hiroshi Yashiro

~Profile~

Name: 渋谷知美(Shibuya Tomomi)

Date of birth: November 9th 1974(Showa 49)

Hometown: Yamamoto town Watari country Miyagi

Age and Sex: 39 years old, woman

Composition of a family: Four families. A husband, 2 girls (8 years old and 4 years old)

About more: When we were living with my parents at my parents' house of Yamamoto town, Watari country, Miyagi, I was caught in an earthquake disaster.

I live in a rental housing provided by company - as a public utility - of Watari town of the neighboring town now. I was working for a swimming school as a part-time instructor three times a week when the earthquake disaster hit. However, because my workplace was destroyed completely, I changed my job. I work as a part-time staff for Yamamoto town reconstruction aid duties now. (Realizing slowed metabolism of my heart and body nowadays… Coffee and avocado are energy sources for me.)

Title: East Japan great earthquake disaster 3.11
Thanks for the support from the United States and the world, thank you for Operation Tomodachi.

February 23 2015

Writer: 渋谷　知美(Shibuya Tomomi)
Publication: HIRO ENTERPRISE Co., Ltd.
Representative director　谷代　浩(Yashiro Hiroshi)
1-4-1-101,Izumihoncho,Komae-shi,Tokyo,201-0003
URL: http://hiroenterprise.net/

Translator　渡邉 舞（Watanabe Mai）
（Thank you Americans, and all the people around the world who have helped us.）
Translator　林　茉以子（Hayashi　Maiko）
Proofreader　吉川 由香利（Yoshikawa Yukari）
Proofreader　山田　泰子（Yamada Yasuko）

COOPERATION
Osaka Noriko / JTCO: The Japanese Traditional Culture Promotion & Development Organization.
URL: http://www.jtco.or.jp/

www.ingramcontent.com/pod-product-compliance
Ingram Content Group UK Ltd.
Pitfield, Milton Keynes, MK11 3LW, UK
UKHW041904190726
13854UKWH00003B/1087